FORMULA
THE GAME OF SALES

ISBN-13:978-1499770407

Published by

DEREK W GRACE
PO Box 154 Ngongota
Rotorua
New Zealand
derekmbc@gmail.com

A publication of

DGrM 🍁

Derek Grace Motivation

DEDICATION

To my mother whose attitude to win has rubbed onto my life. Thank you. And to my father Des Renata who sowed the seed. Thank you.

To my older brothers Amos and David. The trials these men have endured is truly a testimony of courage. Thank you.

To Wayne Stevens who told me, "Never let go of your power." Thank you for being there and believing in me.

To all sales people who determine their own financial future, you are truly brave and exceptional.

To my Creator, your love for me is endless.

To you I dedicate this book.
Thank you.

CONTENT

FORWARD

This book is about the mechanics of selling. The lessons are taken from the life of one of the top door to door sales man of New Zealand, Derek W Grace, of who I had the privilege of mentoring as a young man. I have known Derek since he was a boy and I have watched him develop his amazing gift as a sales man to be a business owner and a motivational speaker. This book captures beautifully his vast experience as a sales man and the life lessons he uses is sure to encourage the new beginner.

Derek was born in Gisborne, a place that is well known for its magnificent beaches, which is situated on the East Coast of the North Island of New Zealand. Derek's journey into the sales world started as a youth of no more than 8 years of age. He has been in the sales and marketing business for twenty years solid. In other words this is his life - selling.

It was in Auckland that Derek started learning how to play the game of sales. His first ever job was selling hamburgers at MacDonald's from whence he launched into door to door selling all over New Zealand, selling just about

THE GAME OF SALES

anything that could be sold from door to door for all sorts of entrepreneurs.

Derek never went to a sales school or even a sales training course. The attraction of an established institution for learning in this business was not the direction for his life having chosen the toughest school in this business - the school of hard knocks and gains, where he learnt his trade. He brings to you his experiences in this book as he learnt it in the field, where every great sales man is birthed.

Richard Meredith
Entrepreneur, Author and Poet

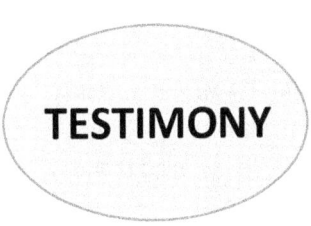

TESTIMONY

My colourful sales career began at the age of 8 years old when I first discovered how to sell and double my money. It all started at a Primary school function where cakes, toffee apples, Candi floss and water melons were on sale, that grabbed the attention of kids running everywhere with excitement.

As I approached each table looking to buy something with 50 cents in my hand, that my mother had given me to spend, I remember thinking to myself, I don't want to spend my 50 cents and at that point I noticed these huge water melon on sale.

If you could picture for a moment a little boy standing in front of a table looking up at water melons. The cost of the water melon was exactly 50 cents. Then this thought entered my little mind, I can buy this water melon for 50 cents cut it up into 10 slices, then sell each slice for 10 cents. I would make my money back and have 50 cents to spend.

With no delay I brought the water melon, ran home with excitement, hurried into the kitchen told mum that I needed to cut up the water melon and why. My mother smiled, and then she cut up my water Melon turned into a family investment. I watched in dismay as my marketing idea dissolve in the mouth of my two older brothers Amos and David. I made up my mind that day, I was going to be a salesman.

However my training to be a sales man came in unexpected way. From the age of 8 years old to leaving school at 13, I had attended over 16 schools, you could say I got pretty good at introducing myself to groups of people I had never met before and by the time I left school I knew how to sell pretty well.

I started in business at the age of 23 years old opening my first restaurant within 3 months, it was a pizzeria. Unfortunately my friends and I ate ourselves out of a business and from that experience I knew I was not cut out to be a chef. With that failed business venture, my sales career then launched.

I answered an advertisement in the local paper, then found myself knocking on doors selling Sky TV door to door, from that point on I went on to brake sales targets after sales target and setting sales bench marks at every company I subsequently worked for.

My most memorable sales experience was selling Cable TV for a huge American firm. During one of our sales meeting, the sales manager of our company together with the company director invited me to explain to the sales team how I managed to top our sales the day before.

I stood up and said like I usually do, 'I go out of my way to please my customers, making them feel at home with me and that is why I sell more units than my companions. I enjoy my job and I pass my joy onto my customers.' As you could imagine the sales team either loved me or hated me because no one loved the job like I did.

The Company manager then told the sales team, that I had sold a cable installation to a couple the day before and when the installers arrived at the address, they asked the couple where the lounge is situated.

The installers then realized there was no TV in the lounge, then they asked the couple what room would they like there cable TV connected, the couple said, "We have no Television but the young man we spoke to yesterday was so enthusiastic and joyful in what he was selling us we decided to join up."

To this day I'm known as the only sales person in New Zealand to have sold Cable TV to a household who did not have a Television!

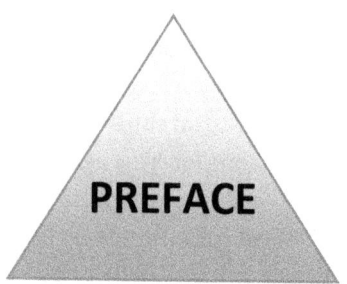

PREFACE

Selling is not just about making money or making a living it is the game of games! A game is defined as a contest with rules to determine a winner. In this game the sellers are the contestants and the buyers are the spectators. The producers provide the product and the rules of the game.

The game starts when one player pitches a presentation of a product or service and it ends when a spectator decides to buy after a floral of negotiations. At the end of the game both parties either win and at time's both lose when they do not play by the producers rules.

Why selling is the game of games is because it is truly the most played game and the universal game of mankind? At any one moment around the world there are more than a billion people playing this game from one corner to the next and from one sunset to the next.

More than 10 trillion dollars are exchanged everyday through this game! It has the highest money stakes of any game that is played on this planet. And best of all anyone can play this game regardless of their social economic status, their religion, their gender or age.

To play this game successfully, you have to know and understand its rules, its moves and its players just like any other game. There are a lot of books and information everywhere about the business of selling but few books will teach its winning rules and plays.

The rules, the plays and examples I will relate in this book are qualified with many experiences and references from other coaches in the game. I have based and centred these lessons in an acronym I have termed the FORMULA from which I will present the learning of this game.

THE MEANING

FORMULA is an acronym for:

Faith **O**vercomes/**R**ejection **M**otivates/**U**nderstanding **L**iberates/**A**lliance

FO/RM/UL/A

FO stands for Faith Overcomes

RM stands for Rejection Motivates

UL stands for Understanding Liberates

A stands for Alliance

FAITH OVERCOMES

The FO of FORMULA demands that we believe we can walk on water; to think the impossible and do the impossible. Developing overcoming faith is the first step to being a successful salesman. Inventor and author Arthur C Clarke said;

> *"It is not enough to just believe in yourself, you have to have **overcoming faith** to be top in your game. The only way of finding the limits of the possible is by going beyond them into the impossible."*

Overcoming faith does not know what a limit or a boundary means. Overcoming faith is always testing and breaking the limits and boundaries that men create. But what exactly is faith that overcomes?

When people think of faith, the first thing they think of is a religion that's because a religion is also called a faith. The word "religion" comes from the Latin word *religio* which means to bind, in the sense of coming into bondage obviously this has nothing to do with faith.

Faith does not produce bondage but it liberates. The word faith comes from the Latin *fides*; akin to Latin *fidere* which means "to trust" and to put it most simply the word trust means to believe in something or someone.

Ralph Waldo Emerson a mid-19th century American philosopher who was the leader of the Transcendentalist movement of the mid-19th century that challenged and broke the boundaries of American literature, philosophy and culture made this statement;

"They can conquer who believe they can."

Similarly Publius Vergilius Maro also known by the Anglicized forms of his name as Virgil known as one of the greatest Roman poets of Pre Christian Rome said,

"They can because they think they can."

You must want to succeed with all of your heart soul and mind and believe with all of your heart soul and mind that you can do this. To think that you can't is to candidly admit to failure before you have even tried. A popular magazine once stated;

"There are three kinds of people in the world, the wills, the won'ts and the can'ts. The first accomplish everything; the second oppose everything; the third fail in everything."
Eclectic Magazine

Everyone comes into this game with many personal handicaps and a history of job disappointments but it is those who believe in themselves that go on to be the success stories in this business.

The first mountain we must conquer is ourselves. This according to Gautama Buddha the founder of Buddhism is a greater task than conquering others.

> *"To conquer oneself is a greater task than conquering others."*

I started in this game with no formal qualification and with no money and many unbelievable handicaps. All I had to go on was the belief that I can do whatever I decide to succeed in. I have always believed in and lived by the motto;

> *"That anything is possible to him who believes"*

Unless you sincerely believe that you can do it, you have barely begun to walk in this game. Becoming a great sales person starts with the belief that you can sell. And if you can believe this, you can achieve it.

FAITH OVERCOMES MEANS BELIEVEING THAT ALL THINGS ARE POSSIBLE.

A couple decided to go to the Caribbean for a holiday but the wife got delayed in her work and had to stay back for 2 days. So the husband said I will go ahead and prepare everything for you. So he did. After two days he sent her an email message but it had one wrong letter in it and it got to another women.

The women who got it is a minister's wife whose husband died 2 days before. As she got the email, the family saw her collapse as she read it.

It read.
From your loving husband.
"Loving greetings from your husband. I have missed you these past few days and you're coming in tomorrow. And I have got to tell you, it is hot down here!"

REJECTION MOTIVATES

The RM of FORMULA demands that we master our fear and make fear work for us. Fear has the potential to become your greatest foe or your greatest ally in this game. The word fear is an acronym for:

False **E**vidence **A**ppearing **R**eal

Fear is an emotion that hides itself in the realm of our imagination, ready to strike at any time like a lion that hides itself to bounce on its prey. After the lion of fear strikes it leaves wounds on the base of our minds that become barriers to our success.

These wounds generate memories and thoughts that become "false evidence" in our psyche. This false evidence appearing real cripples our success when we allow it to dictate to us what we can and what we cannot do. An unknown author wisely cautioned,

"Fear is a darkroom for developing negatives."

It is the development of the negatives into pictures that is printed in the mind that becomes the barriers to our success. We must conquer our fear or fear will surely conquer us. It was President Franklin D Roosevelt during WW11 who said;

"The only thing we have to fear is fear itself."

Selling is a game of unpredictable responses because people are unpredictable. The fear we must conquer above all in this game is the fear of rejection. Let's face it no one likes to be rejected so the quicker you get over it the better for you and your career.

In the game of selling rejection comes with the turf. It is an unavoidable part of the game and the profession. Publius Syrus a writer of maxims, whose writings flourished in the 1st century BCE, brought forth a wisdom for the ages.

"It is idle to dread what you cannot avoid."

Base one in this game requires that you conquer and master the fear of rejection. You must also realize that rejection is ultimately never about failure but about making a success out of failed situations. The Japanese people have a saying,

"Failure teaches success."

In the art of selling a lost sale is never a failure but a spring board from whence one immediately launches into the next sale. When you can turn every instance of failure into a motivation, you have succeeded where very few people know how to succeed. George O. Boule, Jr., successful businessman said,

"Salesmanship starts when the customer says no."

Oliver Goldsmith was an Irish writer, poet, and physician who lived in the 19th Century who experienced failure in many of his personal and business endeavors but he learnt the glory was not in winning but in rising again so he wrote,

"Our greatest glory consist not in never falling, but in rising every time we fall."

When I lost a sale it was a discouragement to me and then I use to avoid going back to where I did not make the sale because of my fear of rejection. Now I consider rejection my motivation and greatest ally.

Unless you can conquer and master your fear you will not make it in this game let alone rise to the top.

REJECTION MOTIVATES MEANS MASTERING THE FEAR OF MAN.

A ten-year-old Jewish boy was failing maths. His parents tried everything from tutors to hypnosis; but to no avail. Finally, at the insistence of a family friend, they decided to enrol their son in a private Catholic school. After the first day, the boy's parents were surprised when he walked in after school with a stern, focused and very determined expression on his face. He went straight past them, right into his room and quietly closed the door. For nearly two hours he toiled away in his room - with math books strewn about his desk and the surrounding floor. He emerged long enough to eat, and after quickly cleaning his plate, went straight back to his room, closed the door and worked feverishly at his studies until bedtime. This pattern of behaviour continued until it was time for the first quarter's report card. The boy walked in with it unopened - laid it on the dinner table and went straight to his room. Cautiously, his Mother opened it and to her amazement, she saw a large red 'A' under the subject of Maths. Overjoyed, she and her husband rushed into their son's room, thrilled at his remarkable progress. "Was it the Nuns that did it?" the father asked. The boy shook his head and said "No". Was it the one-to -one tutoring? The peer-mentoring?" "No" the boy said. The text books? The teachers? The Curriculum?" "No", said the son. "On that first day, when I walked in the front door and saw that guy nailed to the plus sign, I knew they meant business!"

UNDERSTANDING LIBERATES

The UL of FORMULA demands that we understand the game to conquer and fortify against ignorance. Knowledge is power but understanding liberates. Greek philosopher Plato who founded the first academy of learning in the ancient western world said,

"No law or ordinance is mightier than understanding."

When understanding is absent we operate out of the vacuum of ignorance. In the world of sales ignorance is a commodity no one can afford to own because it is a certain and quick road to failure. Philip Wylie an American author summed it up perfectly,

"Ignorance is not bliss — it is oblivion."

In other words when we operate out of ignorance, which is the absence of knowledge it is utter destruction. Chinese philosopher Kung Fu-tzu Confucius founder of

Confucianism defined knowledge as a state of knowing and not knowing.

"The Master said, Yu, shall I tell you what knowledge is? When you know a thing, to know that you know it, and when you do not know a thing, to recognize that you do not know it. That is knowledge."

The first step to acquiring knowledge is to identify what you know and the second being what you do not know. Reading this book is a positive move in filling in the vacuum. 19th Century German Philosopher Friedrich Nietzsche, who wrote critical texts on religion, morality, philosophy and science, likened knowledge to being in a paradise,

"Where there is the tree of knowledge, there is always Paradise..."

The founder and prophet of Islam Muhammad prized knowledge above all other pursuits, he taught his followers to seek knowledge from the cradle to the grave and that it is better to teach knowledge for one hour than to pray all night,

"To spend more time in learning is better than spending more time praying; the support of religion is abstinence. It is better to teach knowledge one hour in the night than to pray all night."

Knowledge of itself is not power unless it is put to practical use. This is a very essential distinction. Dr David. J. Schwartz, author *The Magic of Thinking Big* - American professor, regarded as a foremost expert on motivation and author of several books said,

"Knowledge is power only when put to use — and then only when the use made of it is constructive."

The constructive use of knowledge means knowing the right things to do in this game. Selling is never an enterprise of coincidence or charm but the application of knowledge as successful entrepreneur and writer Stephen A Matuzak wrote,

"Success in your life or business isn't magic or luck — it is the result of knowledge of the right things to do."

In selling knowledge of your product and your competitors business is the mark of a true professional salesman. Bad sales people believe in luck and good sales people believe in cause and effect. As Ralph Waldo Emerson observed,

"Shallow men believe in luck, strong men believe in cause and effect."

My experience in this game has only re-enforced what I have always known – that to succeed at this game one must understand ins and outs of the game. When I first began in this game as an amateur with nothing more than the roof over my head and the clothes on my back. I knew that to make it in this business I had to stop being an amateur and learn the business. As Emerson remarked,

"Every artist was first an amateur."

Unless you are willing to acquire the knowledge of the game you will never experience liberation that understanding brings in the field. You have done well to read this book.

UNDERSTANDING LIBERATES MEANS GETTING EDUCATED IN YOUR FIELD.

A man went fishing on a wharf. Every time he caught a fish he kept throwing it back into the lake and each time he caught a small one he kept it. A mystified bystander, observing his peculiar process of selection asked him what on earth he was doing, with a smile the man replied. "I only have an eighty inch frying pan and so the larger fish won't fit."

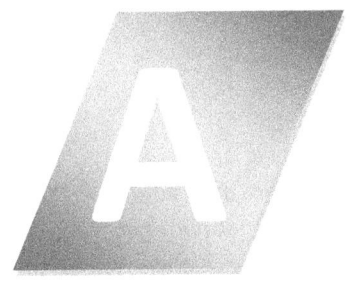

ALLIANCE

The A of FORMULA demands that we learn to be a team of members and to build as a team - a team in this business is a cooperative unit of individuals working together in unison. Founder of the Ford Motor Corporation Henry Ford remarked,

"Coming together is a beginning; keeping together is progress; working together is success."

Every successful business, organisation and institution today is built on the principle of cooperative enterprise. It is the cooperative effort of individual members of the team that brings success to the whole as legendary NFL coach Vincent Lombardi noted,

"Individual commitment to a group effort — that is what makes a team work, a company work, a society work, a civilization work."

Companies stand and fall on the cooperative strength of their sales team. Your chances of success in this game greatly increases when you work as a team as Ford discovered in his beginnings days.

"You will find men who want to be carried on the shoulders of others, who think that the world owes them a living. They don't seem to see that we must all lift together and pull together."

Individual talent is important but to win at this game we must learn to play and stay together. Former professional American football line-backer Ray Bentley who played six seasons with the Buffalo Bills knows what the dividing line between winning and losing.

"There's a very fine line between winning and losing. Every team in the NFL has talent, but attitude is the biggest thing that counts, and playing together as a team. If you can capture that feeling, then you'll have success."

This is the essence of alliance - attitude and feeling, that you are part of a team, and knowing that the team is behind you. Alliance enables the formation of a team matrix that provides a defence against individual failure.

Your failure in a team matrix is totally unacceptable because every dollar you lose weakens the power of the team matrix. When we function as a matrix we avoid being pulled apart. Successful Video producer Bob Allisat said,

"To pull together is to avoid being pulled apart."

To become part of the team matrix you must be prepared to lose your individual spirit and become synonymous with the whole. You must understand that selling is not a business of individual play but of cooperative team work. An ancient proverb captures this principle,

"All organs work together in the functioning of the whole."

In the team matrix no one member in the body is more or less important than the other. Every person in a team matrix is essential and important in the functioning and success of the whole.

In my early sales career I learnt the value of working as a team and it quickly became the reason for the success I enjoyed. I entered the sales world at the age of 15 because I desired like many young people today to be independent but instead I quickly learnt that real success in anything means becoming interdependent. As the age old saying goes,

"United we stand divided we fall."

Unless you are prepared to lose the spirit of individualism and acquire the team attitude you will not breed success let alone taste it.

ALLIANCE MEANS JOINING A TEAM.

Three pastors attended a convention on the power of confession.

They decided to put into action what they had learnt and confessed to one another.

Pastor one said, "I have a problem with lust."
Pastor two said, "I have problem with alcohol."
Pastor three said, "I have problem with gossip and I cannot wait to leave this convention."

BORN TO SELL

A formula is defined as:

> *"A set form of words, as for stating or declaring something definitely or authoritatively, for indicating procedure to be followed, or for prescribed use on some ceremonial occasion or   any fixed or conventional method for doing something."*

Few people realize that is exactly what selling is; Selling is a formula. It is a prescribed set of procedures that we follow, to attain a desired result. The truth is because selling is a formula anyone can learn it regardless of your age, gender or level of education.

Some of the best sellers I have come across in my travels are sadly children in low income countries who sell for survival. They will sell whatever they can acquire for a small profit and they will do it all day and seven days a week in order to survive.

If children know about selling without having to learn it from the sales experts, then it is obvious that anyone can learn or excel in selling. However, what the experts will not tell you is this; you already know how to sell!

The moment you were born you started to learn how to sell and buy. The sooner you realize that selling is an activity we naturally learn in the journey of life, the less incapable you think you are. In fact you are already an innate amateur with the capabilities to make it Big!

Take for example the times in which you tried to convince your father or mother or a sibling or perhaps a friend about something you passionately desired to do or have. Without realizing it what you were doing was selling.

When you got what you wanted, no matter how you like to see it, you had effectively completed a sale irrespective of whether there was any money involved. You see selling is a process of life! We do it all the time instinctively whether you are aware of it or not.

That is why children know and can excel in selling just as any adult can because it is already part of our learning from the time in which we are born. Charles Michael Schwab who was the first president of the US Steel Corporation in 1901 remarked.

"We are all salesmen every day of our lives. We are selling our ideas, our plans, and our enthusiasms to those with whom we come in contact."

Selling is the oldest living occupation and profession in the World. If you are a believer in the Bible you would no doubt realize that selling is what caused the fall or the demise of the human race!

The serpent in the book of Genesis sold Eve, the mother of all mankind, the oldest lie there is in humanity, that we can live forever. The serpent's deceitfulness and Eve's willingness was all that was required to close the first sale's transaction of the human race.

Ever since that moment man has never stopped selling. In fact we all live by it whether you acknowledge it or not. One of the greatest teller of tales Robert Louis Stevenson, author of the famed books, Treasure Island, Robinson Crusoe, Dr Jackal and Hyde agrees;

"Everyone lives by selling something."

This being true then you are quite capable of selling anything. Have your security in your GOD given ability and not your money.

Key Points:

- Selling is a formula.
- Selling is innate in us.
- Selling is a process of life.
- Selling is the oldest occupation.
- Selling is your God given ability.

A man and his wife are awakened at 3 o'clock in the morning by a loud pounding on the door. The man gets up and goes to the door where a drunken stranger standing in a pouring down rain is asking for a push. "Not a chance" says the husband - "It's three o'clock in the morning!" He slams the door and returns to bed.

"Who was it?" asks his wife. "Just a drunken stranger asking for a push" he answers. "Did you help him?" she asks. "No, I didn't -- it's three in the morning and raining like hell out there!" "Well, you've got a short memory" says his wife. "Can't you remember about three months ago when we broke down on the freeway and those two guys helped us? I think you should help him."

The man does as he is told and gets dressed and goes out into the pounding rain and calls out into the dark. "Hello - are you still there?" "Yes," comes the answer.

"Do you still want a push?" calls out the husband.

"Yes, please!" comes the reply from the dark.

"Where are you?" asks the husband.

"Over here on the swing" the drunk replies.

FO2

THE GAME OF FACES

It said that "a picture paints a thousand words" but so does a face. One of my favourite commercials on television is a Red Cross advert that uses a mosaic of faces to make their appeal. German Poet and art critic Rainer Maria Rilke made this insightful statement about our many faces,

> *"I have never been aware before how many faces there are. There are quantities of human beings, but there are many more faces, for each person has several."*

We may be one person but we all have multiple faces that we use at different times. The history of some people can be observed in their face and of some, their present state; it all depends on how you see. In this business we have to learn the game of observing faces to be successful.

In selling the face is the first contact that the customer makes. It will produce the first impression they receive of you and will contribute significantly to the final impression that they make of you. That is because selling is an exchange of emotions.

Creating the first impression even before a word is spoken is more important than you think. Hannah Whitall Smith a leader of the women suffrage and temperance movement of the 19th Century knew all too well the importance of first impressions for she said,

> *"You never get a second chance to make a good first impression."*

Therefore, learn to do it right all the time and the rewards will naturally follow. To be successful and loved in this game, a seller needs to learn how to wake up in the morning with a smile on their face. An unknown author summed it up beautifully,

> *"You are never fully dressed until you wear a smile."*

It is the most important part of your sales attire because,

> *"A little smile adds a great deal to your face value."*

An old proverb

Every sales person has a "face value" that is far more important than any other value attributes he or she may possess, because it is the real stuff that attracts people to you or repels people from you. As these unknown authors observed and wrote;

> *"When you smile, people are drawn to you. When you frown, you repel them."*

"The shortest distance between new friends is a smile."

"A smile is a light in the window of the soul indicating that the heart is at home."

Generally speaking successful sales people are generally happy people, because they have to be in order to make it in this game, why who would want to buy anything from a grumpy sales man, would you? Having said that I would like to personally invite you to join the happy gang!

The happy gang has but one rule and motto by which new members must swear by in order to be initiated into the club. You must smile at least 10 times a day. You will be surprised on how such an insignificant act will transform your sales career let alone your life.

"A smile is a curve that sets everything straight."

Unknown author

If this is true, then you are quite capable of becoming a fantastic sales person. Are you ready to be initiated into the happy gang?

Key Points:

- Selling starts with the right face.
- Selling is an exchange of emotions.
- Sales people have a face value.
- Sales people know customers prefer happy faces.
- Sales people are generally happy people.

A man said to his wife, "Why are you so beautiful and dumb?"
She answered "God made me beautiful so that you would look at me and dumb, so that I would say yes to you when you asked me to marry you."

THE LOOK OF THE GAME

It has been said many times over 'that people will do just about anything to make a buck these days.' It is not unusual these days to come across sales people dressed in all sorts of funny or strange looking outfits to attract a sale.

Take for instance the enormously successful Santa Claus outfit that many sales people wear around the period of November-December to attract people to their establishment. Who has not been taken in by these Santa outfits at one point in their life?

Business owners know that people are attracted by what they see first. That's why they are prepared to spend exuberant amounts of money on producing and airing expensive Television adverts because they know it works. Our eyes more often than our ears do most of the leading in our lives.

A recent survey conducted in America found that consumers in the USA had a better opinion of products that they saw on television, than products that they did not see advertised. They trusted products that were advised more than the ones that were not.

This is not a coincident. People are moved by what they see. When you translate this to a personal level, people simply will not buy if they are not attracted to you as a person. That is why sales people are prepared to look ridiculous or lavishing to generate sales.

This all has to do with the game of styles. A style is more than just "a look" it has to do with our mannerism, the way we speak, the way we dress, the way we move and the way we feel. It all counts towards the customer's final assessment before making the sale.

It is not unusual for a customer to reject a sale because they simply did not like the way you spoke, the way you walked, the manner you responded, or even the tie you wore on that day. People respond differently according to how they relate to you.

The look of the game is all about learning how to relate to others. This directly translates into how you perform financially and whether you will get repeated business or not. As former IBM manager, sales director and author Dan Brent Burt observed,

"The better you relate the more you will make."

There is simply no magic in this game, there is no casting of spells, good luck charms or amulets that is going to influence the result. To be successful at this game you must learn to do those things that are going to make you into the sales person you dream to be.

As Dan Brent Burt rightly observed,

"Every boxer fights differently, and every salesman has his unique style. But the results are the same— you are either a champion or just another fighter, you get the sale or you don't. The real key to success is to do those things that will prepare you to be a champion."

If the key lies in doing those things that will prepare us to be a champion then you have got to get the right look or make the look right.

Key Points:

- Sales people know people are attracted by what they see.
- Sales people know advertising create customer confidence.
- Sales people are prepared to do what it takes to succeed.
- Selling is about relating to others.
- Selling is about the right look.

A bald man took a seat in a beauty shop. "How can I help you?" asked the stylist. "I went for a hair transplant." The guy explained, "But I couldn't stand the pain. If you can make my hair look like yours without causing me any discomfort, I'll pay you $5,000." "No problem," said the stylist, and she quickly shaved her head.

Debbie Costet

SELL TO SUCCEED

There are three laws to selling;

> *"See more people, see more people and see more people."*

The odds lessen in this game when the numbers go up. The more people we see the better the numbers become for you and the boss. There is no other rule in the world of selling that sets the stats than this universal law – see more people!

At the end of the business day, it all comes down to performance and numbers. Bosses want to see results and sellers want to earn more commissions and that's business! In this game it's all about seeing people. As Dan Brent Burt remarked;

> *"Selling is a people business."*

People and not money is the sunshine of your career. The more people you meet and prospect, the greater the sunshine. The fewer people you meet and prospect, the cloudier it becomes. You must be prepared to clock the hours.

A 52 hour week for a sales person and meeting over 100 customers a week is normal and to be expected. Sales people are hardworking people, they are not afraid of hard work because they know the commitment it takes to succeed in this game.

In order to harvest from this field, we must daily plough the ground and plant our seed. Prospecting people in our minds (dreaming of a sale) and not doing the hard work will not get you anywhere in this business. As this unknown author correctly observed,

> *"You cannot plough a field by turning it over in your mind."*

Selling is not a place for dreamers; it is a place for a realist who wants to win with all of their heart. We may never make top sales man of the firm but wanting to win is everything. As legendary football coach of the Green Bay packagers Vince Lombardi once said,

> *"Winning isn't everything, but wanting to win is."*

To excel at this game you must make selling a habit. The oxford dictionary defines a habit as *"a settled tendency or practice."* In other words it is something that we repeatedly do day in and day out. According to Greek philosopher Aristotle this is what defines us.

"We are what we repeatedly do. Excellence, therefore, is not an act but a habit."

Sales people are not defined by their talent or abilities, but by what they do day in and day out. It is the sum of these daily efforts no matter how insignificant that make a sales person a success or a failure. American writer and author Robert Collier summed it up perfectly,

"Success is the sum of small efforts, repeated day in and day out."

Author and radio personality Sterling W. Sill who wrote *"How to Personally Profit From the Laws of Success,"* agrees,

"Successful people follow successful patterns."

If you make selling a lifestyle then success will naturally beat a path to your door as a river would beat a path to the ocean.

Key Points:

- Sales people know that the success of this game is in the numbers.
- Sales people know that selling can be long hours.
- Sales people know that wanting to win is everything.
- Selling must be a habit.
- Selling must be a lifestyle.

A sales man and his wife were having some problems at home and were giving each other the silent treatment.

The next day the man realized that he would need his wife to wake him at 5 am for an early flight to Sydney. Not wanting to be the first to break the silence, he finally wrote on a piece of paper, "Please wake me at 5 am."

The next morning the man woke up, only to discover it was 9 am, and that he had missed his flight!

Furious, he was about to go and see why his wife hadn't awakened him when he noticed a piece of paper by the bed. It said, "Its 5 am, wake up."

THE GAME OF ATTITUDE

Attitude is all about the way we think. Our attitude is a reflection of our character which is manifested in our conduct and in our speech. Attitude has a lot to do with this game because it directly affects your performance as a sales person.

M. Russell Ballard an American Business man and Apostle of the Church of Jesus Christ of Latter Day Saints, ranks attitude as the most influential factor in determining the shape of our life and I cannot agree more.

"We each shape our own life, and the shape of it is determined largely by our attitude."

Customers sense our attitude; that is they can feel our thoughts. When our thinking stinks or it has a pleasant aroma, they can smell it. In the world of sales attitude is everything because it affects everything. As Sterling W. Sill wrote,

"Everything depends on attitude. We are ambitious or lazy, enthusiastic or dull, loyal or undependable, according to our attitude. We get good grades or poor grades — according to our attitudes. Discouragement is an attitude. Lack of industry is an attitude. Failure to follow instructions is an attitude."

When our attitude is pleasant and pleasing to others we attract people who in turn become a customer who in turn become a sale. Many of us have heard about the law of attraction which simply stated says that, *"like attracts like or like begets like."*

In other words your attitude will either repel or attract prosperity. It is very easy to recognize a sales person, who has the great attitude, they are never alone! People are attracted to their personality and they make people feel right at home.

That is because the right attitude sees the customer as a person and not a sale. As a person they are important and demand to be respected no matter their gender, age or social economic status. As former IBM manager, sales director Dan Brent Burt said,

"Specialize in making others feel important."

Bosses never tire with employees who have a great attitude and it does not take long before their kind is promoted. A great attitude will always amplify your prospects. It was Paul H Dunn, a dynamic speaker and motivator of the 70s and 80s who first said,

"Our attitude determines our altitude."

When your attitude is right any target, goal or objective are only steps in a ladder that you climb in your day. Numbers and figures are simply the rewards of a well worked day and never the purpose of the day. The purpose of the day is to enjoy what you do.

There is nothing more repulsive in this game than a person who has a bad attitude. People avoid there kind like they would avoid the plague. Therefore, if you can change anything improve your attitude. Again quoting from Dan Brent Burt,

"If you could change anything about the way you approach selling, the thing that will make the biggest difference would be your attitude — your attitude toward your customers, your service, the benefits of your products, your employer, and yourself."

Some sales people when you meet them, drain you and some sales people immediately energize you. The difference is, a great attitude and that my friend is the nature of a great sales man.

If there is anything you can do today to prepare yourself for this game or improve your sales game is to change or reform your attitude.

Key Points:

- Selling is about having the right attitude.
- Sales people enjoy what they do.
- Sales people know that wanting to win is the right attitude.

A man had two twin boys. On their sixth birthday he played a game on them. On the morning of their birthday he took one son into a room full of toys and the other son into a room full of manure. After an hour he returned to check on his two sons. The son who had a room full of toys to his surprise was sobbing. With tears in his eyes he said to his father "I cannot get these toys to work properly and I don't like many of them." The father then proceeded to check on the other son. To his surprise the son who was in the room full of manure on seeing him ran and embraced his legs and said, "Dad! Where is the pony I looked everywhere for it?"

LOVE OF THE GAME

Love of the game is all about enjoying what you do. We do a lot of different things in life for different purposes but nothing compares to those things we do which brings us personal enjoyment. When we enjoy what we do, time and money become secondary issues.

On the contrary when we dislike what we do, time and money is of the primary issue. Samuel Butler was an English novelist who wrote many literary works in the 19th Century, this is a man who clearly understood the value of enjoying what you do.

> *"Most people have never learned that one of the main aims in life is to enjoy it."*

For the majority of people their occupation/vocation is there life. Their job defines who they are and what they are, the job in essence becomes their very purpose in life but the question you need to ask yourself is; does that purpose bring you enjoyment?

Some people work just for the money, others for survival and still others for the challenge but whatever the motive may be, without a genuine love for what you do, the job in the end becomes "just another job." Selling must be a passion.

To avoid the syndrome of "just another job" from happening to you, it is important that you make it your goal to love what you do, because if you don't the work that you do will become a load and a burden that is sure to quickly wear you out. Billionaire Warren Buffer in addressing a class of students at the University of Nebraska reportedly said;

"If there is any difference between you and me, it may simply be that I get up every day and have a chance to do what I love to do, every day. If you want to lean anything from me, this is the best advice I can give you."

This is the secret of purposeful and effortless employment - when you love the job you do, the hard work or repetitive tasks involved becomes effortless because you now work for the enjoyment it personally brings you. This unknown author hit it on the head,

"When you find a job you love, you'll never have to work a day in your life."

This is the "occupation utopia" that few people ever discover in their working life. The more you enjoy the work that you do the harder you want to work, to the point where it no longer seems to be work at all.

Sure every sales person has a bad day once in a while, but if you have job enjoyment even the bad days will have a measure of satisfaction because love of the job overcomes all things. Interestingly online Wikipedia describes job satisfaction as,

"... How content an individual is with his or her job. The happier people are within their job, the more satisfied they are said to be."

The link between Job enjoyment and Job satisfaction is an established fact. The undeniable truth is it is very hard to succeed at a job in which you do not enjoy even if your motives are honorable and good. A proverb states,

"Few people succeed at anything unless they enjoy it."

Finally here is some great advice from Malcolm S. Forbes publisher of Forbes Magazine;

"Working at what you enjoy is far more important than what you're working at."

Therefore do as the great Minnesota politician and lobbyist Gerry Sikorski suggested;

"Be absolutely determined to enjoy what you do."

Key Points:

- Sales people love what they do.
- Selling is not a job but a passion.
- Sale people see selling as fun.

At the end of their first date, a young man takes his favourite girl home. Emboldened by the night, he decides to try for that important first kiss. With an air of confidence, he leans with his hand against the wall and, smiling, he says to her,

"Darling, how 'bout a goodnight kiss?" Horrified, she replies, "Are you mad? My parents will see us!" "Oh come on! Who's going to see us at this hour?" "No, please. Can you imagine if we get caught?" "Oh come on, there's nobody around, they're all sleeping!" "No way. It's just too risky!" "Oh please, please, I like you so much!!" "No, no, and no. I like you too, but I just can't!" "Oh yes you can. Please?" "NO, no. I just can't." "Pleeeeease?"

Out of the blue, the porch light goes on, and the girl's sister shows up in her pyjamas, hair dishevelled. In a sleepy voice the sister says: "Dad says to go ahead and give him a kiss. Or I can do it. Or if need be, he'll come down himself and do it. But for crying out loud tell him to take his hand off the intercom button!"

KNOW YOUR PRODUCT

Selling a product you do not know anything about is tantamount to misrepresentation. It is our law abiding responsibility as a seller to know what we are representing. The online Wikipedia defines misrepresentation as;

"Misrepresentation is a contract law concept. It means a false statement of fact made by one party to another party, which has the effect of inducing that party into the contract. For example, under certain circumstances, false statements or promises made by a seller of goods regarding the quality or nature of the product that the seller has may constitute misrepresentation. A finding of misrepresentation allows for a remedy of rescission and sometimes damages depending on the type of misrepresentation."

Thus, it is your legal responsibility as a law abiding sales person to find out all you can about the product you are selling and I am not referring to general information. You need to find out the following important and essential facts;

- The products place and year of manufacture,
- It's warranty offer and claims,
- It's sales terms and conditions,
- It's operating requirements, does it need batteries, water, power etc.,
- It's used by date or other important auxiliary information,
- What it actually does and offers the customer.

The more facts you can accumulate about what it is you are selling, the better equipped you will be at answering your customer questions and best of all avoiding misrepresentation. It is also a matter of good seller's conscience (good ethics) to speak the truth to others.

The fact of the matter is selling something without a "clear conscience" of its specifics never works in this business because it does not result in repeat business or referrals, which is the bottom line to being successful in this game.

The word is sure to get around and both your customers and your competitors will use your blunders to the max to discredit you and your company. It always pays in both the short and long term to play an honest game with people. As writer and author Mark Twain said,

"Honesty is the best policy — when there is money in it."

Now that I have got your attention about being a conscientious sales person there are some things you need to understand why people buy a product. There are many myths that people circulate about product knowledge. Here are the three most common myths and the response of the experts to these myths:

Myth One – it's the product

(1) *"**People buy product for what they can do**, not for what they are."*

F. G. 'Buck' Rodgers - *IBM sales trainee 1950, vice president of marketing 1974, author, leadership trainer.*

Myth Two – it's the quality

"Quality in a product or service is not what the supplier puts in. It is what the customer gets out and is willing to pay for. A product is not quality because it is hard to make and costs a lot of money, as manufacturers typically believe. This is incompetence. (2) ***Customers pay only for what is of use to them and gives them value. Nothing else constitutes quality.***"

Peter F. Drucker - *US management professor, NY University, advisor to world's business & government, 'the dean of management'.*

Finally,

Myth Three – it's the price

(3) *"**Ninety seven percent of customers are sold price but only three percent buy price**. It is fact"*

Gerald A Michaelson with Steven W Michaelson - *Tzun Tzu Strategies for Selling*

Key Points:

- Sales people know what they are selling.
- Sales people are educated on their business.
- Selling is knowing the facts and the fallacies.

A businessman was having trouble with his sales. So he called in a consultant to give him an objective view and some good advice. After he had explained all of his plans and problems, he showed the consultant a map into which he had stuck brightly coloured pins wherever he had a salesman. Then he said, "O.K., for starter, what is the first thing we should do?" "Well," said the consultant, "the first thing is to take those pins out of the map and stick them in the salesmen."

Erick W Johnson, a Treasury of Humour 11

UNDERSTAND YOUR COMPETITION

No matter what areas of selling you decide to work in or what level of selling you operate in there will be competition. Smart sales people do the smart thing and take their time to find out who their competitors are and what are their strengths and weaknesses.

In marketing literature this is called a Competitor Analysis and is defined in Wikipedia as;

> *"Competitor analysis ...is an assessment of the strengths and weaknesses of current and potential competitors."*

The reason why this is an important and essential part of the selling game is because it is all about formulating sales and marketing strategies to give a business owner and sales people an advantage in the market. Again referring to Wikipedia;

> *"This analysis provides both an offensive and defensive strategic context through which to identify opportunities*

and threats. Competitor profiling coalesces all of the relevant sources of competitor analysis into one framework in the support of efficient and effective strategy formulation, implementation, monitoring and adjustment."

In simpler terms it means gathering knowledge of your rivals, business so that you can have the "competitive advantage" as others would put it "being a step ahead of your competitors". He who possesses the competitive advantage will sell the most and make the most.

Make it your business to find out periodically what your competitors are offering, where they are selling and whom they are targeting. Every effective strategy depends on what the competition is doing. As business entrepreneur D. Henderson remarked,

"All strategy depends on competition."

Competition is no gentlemen's game either. Make no mistake about this! It's a world of where your rivalries are always trying to outdo or kill you. That's because there is only so much room in the market for X amount of players and three is always a crowd.

Successful sales people thrive on competition. The harder the competition the harder they attack the market. Here are some examples of what successful business people think about their competition. And notice who said it.

"You either eat someone for lunch, or you can be lunch."

Scott McNealy, *CEO of Sun Microsystems*

"Competition is a way of life. If you don't have a really tough competitor, you ought to invent one."

Roberto Goizueta, *CEO of Coca-Cola*

"I don't meet competition. I crush it."

Charles Haskell Revlon - *US cosmetics businessman; founder and 1st president of Revlon, Inc. 1932-1962.*

"If any of my competitors were drowning, I'd stick a hose in their mouth."

"This is rat eat rat, dog eat dog. I'll kill 'em, and I'm going to kill 'em before they kill me. Speaking of competition in the fast-food industry."

Ray Kroc *US founder & chairman of McDonalds Corporation., revolutionized fast food industry.*

You are not in this game to play the nice guy because you can bet your last dollar on this fact that your competition will be finding out all they can in order to outsmart you, outsell you, outperform you and finally if they can terminate you! So don't get offended by Mr. Kroc's remark he is absolutely right!

In my backyard every day there were three to four other companies selling the same or similar products in my business, often in the same town and in the same streets, but the difference with my success was that I had formulated a strategy that killed my opposition. I would tell my reps to tell people that we are the only company in town that helped the local community.

Selling is a game of war and war as British Philosopher, historian and social critic Bertrand Russell intuitively surmised;

"War does not determine who is right - only who is left."

Key Points:

- Sales people know that selling is competitive.
- Selling is about having the right strategy.
- Sales people know their competition.
- Sales people thrive on competition.
- Selling is a game of war.

The salesman was showing his prospect through a house. Everything was fine until the prospect glanced up at the ceiling and found unmistakably obvious signs of water damage. "It's a bit damp, isn't it?" he asked. "Damp!" the salesman enthused. "Of course it's damp. Just think what an advantage that would be in case of fire!"

Good Reading

PERFECT YOUR PRESENTATION

Products do not sell of themselves. An Intrinsic part of selling is the sales presentation. A sales presentation is a salesman's effort to make a sale. It can be as simple as a one minute introduction to one hour long talk.

The lone exception to the sales representation is where a customer has been directly referred to you by another customer in which case most of the time the customer has already decided to buy and the impending discussion will be to find out how you may best fill the customer's need.

A sales presentation is designed to convince a potential buyer to consider and commit to purchase a product or service that they would otherwise not buy. The core of a sales presentation is the sales pitch. A sale pitch is defined by Wikipedia as,

"... A planned presentation of a product or service designed to initiate and close a sale of the same product or service. A sales pitch is essentially designed to be either an introduction of a product or service to an audience who knows nothing about it, or a descriptive expansion of

THE GAME OF SALES

*a product or service that an audience has already
expressed interest in."*

The key to a successful sales pitch is "content", where content is defined as information and experiences that will provide value and incentive for a buyer to commit to a sale.

Well researched and well qualified presentations make a tremendous difference to a buyer. However, the less words you use in your sales pitch, makes you look like a sales genius. So keep it short and simple.

Buyers are looking for reasons why they should choose your product and not your competitors. It is therefore the goal of the sales presentation to impact the buyer. However, content alone will not do the job.

In the market today we are also facing a different breed of consumer. The "sophisticate" who generally knows what they want and what is available in the market because of the proliferation of advertisements from the media.

This has made the market much more "salesman driven" requiring that buyers be pitched for a sale. Not so long ago the majority of consumers use to buy on price but with the availability of "finance" and "terms" the game has radically changed. Sale's executive and motivational speaker John Gifford made this statement of which shows how consumers have shifted in their perspective in the market.

*"While that's still true, price objective has moved down to
fourth or fifth for buyers. Now the appeal is for
presentation, excitement, a differentiated product,
something that is unique and entertaining."*

58 | P a g e

Consumers today are looking for innovative sales pitches that will both persuade them and make them feel important. The best sales presentations are therefore interactive and anticipatory. The Lilyan Wilder Centre for Communications noted,

> *"You want to keep getting responses throughout your presentation.* ***The more give and take and the more interactive it is, the better****."*

It must also anticipate the responses of your buyer as writer Arthur Helps noted.

> *"The very best ... presentation is one that's well thought out and* ***anticipates any questions... answering them in advance****."*

This demands above all that a sales person knows how to communicate. Communication is the single most important skill that a sales man requires to prosper in this field – something that we learn and perfect along the way. As expert salesman Dan Brent Burt remarked,

> *"The single most important tool in selling is being able to communicate effectively."*

Key Points:

- Sales people know they need to pitch their product.
- Sales people understand how to pitch their products.
- Sales people understand they must impact the customer.
- Selling is about knowing how to communicate.

Hymn #365

A minister was completing a temperance sermon. With great emphasis he said,
"If I had all the beer in the world, I'd take it and pour it into the river."
With even greater emphasis he said, "And if I had all the wine in the world, I'd take it and pour it into the river."
And then finally, shaking his fist in the air, he said, "And if I had all the whiskey in the world, I'd take it and pour it into the river."
Sermon complete, he sat down. The song leader stood very cautiously and announced with a smile, nearly laughing, "For our closing song, Let us sing Hymn #365, 'Shall We Gather at the River.'"

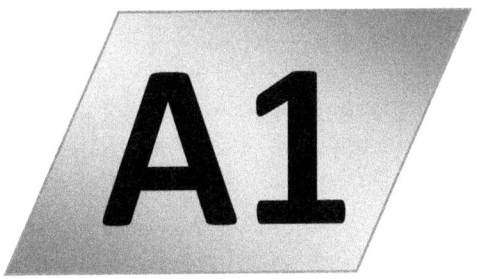

GIVE ENTHUSIASM

The success of alliance lies in its power to create enthusiasm. Where there is a team attitude there will be a natural reservoir of enthusiasm – an energy reserve of positive emotion that is created when people decide to work together instead of competing with each other.

Successful business managers know how to create this energy. Walter Chrysler founder of the Chrysler Corporation, one of the top three biggest automobile manufacturers in the World revealed his secret of success when he said,

> *"The real secret of success is enthusiasm."*

Charles Schwab founder of the Charles Schwab Corporation, one of the largest discount brokers and investment firms in the World agrees,

"A man can succeed at almost anything for which he has unlimited enthusiasm."

This is what team attitude brings to the game of sales – an unlimited supply of enthusiasm of which is the life line of any business. Enthusiasm always translates into team support of which is essential in achieving a business's sales goals and targets.

Where there is team support their will be individual support. Consider when one person is not performing as they should in a team, another team member is always there to chastise, encourage or motivate the non performing member of the team.

You will not find this motivation anywhere when sales is an individual pursuit. Where there is an absence of enthusiasm the impeding result is always the same. Legendary NFL coach Vincent Lomabrdi put it this way,

"If you aren't fired with enthusiasm, you will be fired with enthusiasm."

Enthusiasm is the life blood of the soul. When the soul runs out of enthusiasm it lacks the energy to work. The result is every hill you climb will become a mountain and every creek you cross becomes a river. As motivational guru Norman Vincent Peale said,

"Years wrinkle the skin, but lack of enthusiasm wrinkles the soul."

You may hold a qualification in education or marketing which helps but without a source or reservoir of enthusiasm that knowledge will not guarantee you success in this game. There is an invisible connection that has to be made as Poet and writer Ivern Ball wrote,

"Knowledge is power, but enthusiasm pulls the switch."

Knowledge plus enthusiasm is the fuel for innovation, creativity and drive. There is simply no limit to what can be achieved when you have knowledge and enthusiasm combined and it thrives where people decide to work together as a unit but then selling is not always a team thing.

Better still become a person who imparts to others enthusiasm and watch that energy return back to you as a tenfold or hundredfold harvest. Every Christian is familiar with this verse from the Bible and rightly so.

"Give, and it will be given to you: good measure, pressed down, shaken together, and running over will be put into your bosom. For with the same measure that you use, it will be measured back to you."

Key Points:

- Sales people know to be successful at this game you must possess enthusiasm.
- Sales people understand you must have a reservoir of energy to be a success at this game.
- Selling is about giving others enthusiasm.

A little boy was overheard praying: "Lord, if you can't make me a better boy, don't worry about it. I'm having a real good time like I am."

I had been teaching my three-year old daughter, Caitlin, the Lord's Prayer for several evenings at bedtime, she would repeat after me the lines from the prayer. Finally, she decided to go solo. I listened with pride as she carefully enunciated each word, right up to the end of the prayer:
"Lead us not into temptation," she prayed, "but deliver us some E-mail. Amen."

A Sunday school teacher asked her children, as they were on the way to church service, "And why is it necessary to be quiet in church?
One bright little girl replied, "Because people are sleeping."

Six-year-old Angie and her four-year-old brother Joel were sitting together in church. Joel giggled, sang, and talked out loud. Finally, his big sister had had enough.
"You're not supposed to talk out loud in church."
"Why? Who's going to stop me?" Joel asked. Angie pointed to the back of the church and said, "See those two men standing by the door? They're hushers."

VALUE SERVICE

Buyers are no longer satisfied with just getting a good product, they expect good service and when we fail to provide that service they cry "foul play!" even when the product they have bought meets their requirements. That is because the market today is consumer orientated.

"Consumer Orientation is the focus on meeting the needs of one's customers, internal or external. This service establishes specific customer satisfaction standards and actively monitors client satisfaction, taking steps to clarify and meet customer needs and expectations (both expressed and unexpressed). At lower levels the service involves courteous and timely responsiveness to the requests of customers, while at the higher levels, it involves developing the relationship of partner and trusted advisor."

http://wiki.answers.com/Q/What_is_consumer_orientati on#ixzz16E4n3L2Z

Satisfying the needs of the customer is what drives marketing and sales strategy. Business owners know that a dissatisfied customer will not amount to repeat business or create customer referrals of which is vital to getting repeat or new business.

When buyers speak today of getting a "good deal" they mean that they are satisfied with the product they bought and service they received. Both the product and the service constitute the deal in the mind of consumers. Entrepreneur Hugh W. Coburn explains,

"Modern business requires that its salesmen be business men in the best sense of the word—men who know the ins and outs of the product or service they are selling ... men who can make an intelligent and effective presentation ... and most of all, men who have the modern concept of service to the customer."

Notice the statement "and most of all" pointing to customer service as being the single most important requirement to a customer. Customer service is defined as "the provision of service to customers before, during and after a purchase."

These three stages of a purchase are interconnected. The service a business provides after purchase is just as important, if the after sales support fails it all reflects back on the seller who sold the product to the buyer in the first instance.

Much of the after sale problems that can occur can be eliminated by developing good customer relationship as Dan Brent Burt noted,

"By developing strong customer relationships the little problems that could arise in the selling process seem to take care of themselves."

The key to developing a strong customer relationship is primarily about being honest with your "representations" to the customer before the sale. Former director and vice president of marketing for IBM F. G. 'Buck' Rodgers gave this sober advice,

"Don't make misrepresentations to anyone you deal with. If you believe the other person may have misunderstood you, correct any misunderstanding you find exists. Honesty is integral to ethical behaviour, and trustworthiness is essential for good, lasting relationships."

Successful sales people do not manufacture untruths or create hype to sell their products or services they offer. They believe in their products and in their services because they already know what they are selling is good and the services they are providing is good.

The customer on the other hand leaves the transaction knowing that they too have bought something good and have received good service. All because the customer believed the sales person was honest and sincere in his or her presentations.

I have always said that, I would rather have one happy customer than ten unhappy buyers.

Key Points:

- Sales people know the market is consumer orientated.
- Sales people understand their business is about customer satisfaction.
- Selling entails integrity.
- Selling is about customer service.
- Selling is about customer satisfaction.

Zorbat Dukakis, a wealthy art dealer, discovers he has terminal illness. Zorba call his three best friends, a doctor, a priest and a lawyer, and gives them $500,000 apiece. He tells them, "I know I can't take it with me, but I want to try. I want your assurance that you will put this $500,000 cash into my casket at my funeral and have it buried with me." A month later, Zorba died and following the funeral, the three friends got together. The doctor said, "I've got to confess, I didn't put the money in the casket. I gave it to the hospital foundation to build a new children's wing." The priest said, "I've got to confess too. I didn't put that $500,000 in the casket either. I gave it to the Little Sisters of the Poor to build a new treatment centre at the nursing home." Well I'm aghast. I just want you to know that he was buried with my personal cheque for $500,000 in his casket!"

Nelson's Big book of Laughter

BE MOTIVATED

Successful sales people are highly motivated people. They have to be in order to survive and prosper in this game. But what exactly is motivation? Remez Sasson of Success Consciousness.Com offers this basic definition,

"Motivation is the inner power or energy that pushes toward acting, performing actions and achieving."

In the business of sales being motivated is the greatest personal asset one can have. Any sales executive will tell you that it is far more important in this business to have motivation than talent as this proverb states.

"Intense motivation is a more important commodity than talent."

Talent is useful and can be an advantage but not important enough to outweigh the benefit of plain motivation. That is because sale executives know it is motivated people who get the job done and get the results that business owners are looking for. Talent is only a bonus.

To possess motivation one must have a desire and ambition to succeed, and if they are absent, motivation is absent too. Formula one Italian born racing legend Mario Andretti won many coveted trophies in his sport, he knows what it takes to achieve success.

To Mario desire is the key but it is sheer determination, commitment and pursuit of one's goals that is the winning combination. What Mario calls *"a commitment to excellence"* that distinguishes a winner?

> *"Desire is the key to motivation, but **its determination and commitment to an unrelenting pursuit of your goal** — a commitment to excellence — that will enable you to attain the success you seek."*

Successful sales people are never satisfied with the status quo; they are constantly testing the limits of their own achievements and that of others. Harold R. McAlindon author of *the little book of Big ideas* offers this advice,

> *"Do not follow where the path may lead. Go instead where there is no path and leave a trail."*

To borrow a phrase from the Star Trek series motivated people *"go where no man has gone before"* and they leave a blazing trail for others to follow. To become a trail blazer you must stop being a follower and learn to take the initiative. To do this you must realize that;

In this game 'time' is never a factor because there is never a wrong time for a great deal. There is always someone ready for a great deal because statistics show that consumers needs and wants never abate or stop growing. Consumerism is a thriving animal.

In this game condition are never perfect, the customer will never be in the right mood or the right place to make the deal. The conditions are always right to make a deal and if they are difficult we must do as the great American Union General William B. Sprague said,

> *"Do not wait to strike till the iron is hot; but make it hot by striking."*

A little more than two years ago I had the opportunity to make a presentation to a team of sales people that worked for a company. I was surprised to learn that many of the people that worked at this company have never before been in the sales game but they were exceptionally motivated because they had a boss who was himself highly motivated and believed in them.

There is however a final stage to your evolution as a top sales person. You must endeavour to make selling a habit in your life. As motivational expert Dr David. J. Schwartz taught it's all about getting *"the action habit."*

> *"Get the action habit — you do not need to wait until conditions are perfect."*

When selling becomes part of your psychology and your way of life everything else will come naturally to you and you will never need to pursue success because success will pursue you and overtake you.

Key Points:

- Sales people know that the sales game is about motivation.
- Sales people know it is motivated people who get the job done.
- Sales people understand that a desire and ambition to succeed is essential.
- Sales people create their own trail.
- Selling is never about the right time. It is always the right time to make a deal.
- Selling must become a habit.

A businessman was having trouble with his sales. So he called in a consultant to give him an objective view and some good advice. After he had explained all of his plan and problems, he showed the consultant a map into which he had stuck brightly coloured pins wherever he had a salesman. Then he said, "O.K., for a starter, what is the first thing we should do?" "Well," said the consultant, "the first thing is to take those pins out of the map and stick them in the salesmen."

Eric W Johnson, a Treasury of Hummor11

SUMMARY

FORMULA is not a guarantee of success; it is the WAY of success. FORMULA is the narrow way of where successful players are going that makes them the winners and leaders they are in this game. It is the winner's way and there is no other way.

FORMULA is not a formulae for success; it is the PATTERN of success. FORMULA is the blueprint of how successful players are behaving that makes them the winners and leaders that are in this game. Successful players follow successful patterns.

FORMULA is not magic for success; it is the WORK of success. FORMULA is the workings of what successful players are doing that makes them the winners and leaders that are in this game. It is doing the right things that bring the success.

FORMULA is an acronym for:

Faith Overcomes/Rejection Motivates/Understanding Liberates/Alliance

Faith Overcomes is the Power and Inspiration of this game. It is belief in yourself and trust in your abilities that will propel you to the top of this game. Learning the simple things of the game like to smile and have the right look improves your play.

Rejection Motivates is the Mountain and Valley of this game. It is the obstacles that stand in our way that stop us from excelling in this game. For most it is the fear of rejection and failure and the wrong attitude which we must overcome to win in this game.

Understand Liberates is the Knowledge and Understanding of this game. Ignorance of your product, presentation and competition will give away the advantage. The winning combination is to understand your strengths and the weakness of the competition.

Alliance is the Foundation of this game. It is working and moving together as a team that is the way to win in this game. Where there is a team spirit there is, service, motivation and enthusiasm. It is hard to loose in this game when you have that behind you.

TERMINOLOGY

A Game is a contest with rules to determine a winner.

Formula is a set form of words, as for stating or declaring something definitely or authoritatively, for indicating procedure to be followed, or for prescribed use on some ceremonial occasion or any fixed or conventional method for doing something.

A Team is a cooperative unit of individuals working together in unison.

Consumer Orientation is the focus on meeting the needs of one's customers, internal or external. This service establishes specific customer satisfaction standards and actively monitors client satisfaction, taking steps to clarify and meet customer needs and expectations (both expressed and unexpressed). At lower levels the service involves courteous and timely responsiveness to the requests of customers, while at the higher levels, it involves developing the relationship of partner and trusted advisor.

The Sale pitch is a planned presentation of a product or service designed to initiate and close a sale of the same product or service. A sales pitch is essentially designed to be either an introduction of a product or service to an audience who knows nothing about it or a descriptive expansion of a product or service that an audience has already expressed interest in.

Content is information and experiences that will provide value and incentive for a buyer to commit to a sale.

Competitor analysis is an assessment of the strengths and weaknesses of current and potential competitors.

Misrepresentation is a contract law concept. It means a false statement of fact made by one party to another party, which has the effect of inducing that party into the contract. For example, under certain circumstances, false statements or promises made by a seller of goods regarding the quality or nature of the product that the seller has may constitute misrepresentation. A finding of misrepresentation allows for a remedy of rescission and sometimes damages depending on the type of misrepresentation.

Job satisfaction is how content an individual is with his or her job. The happier people are within their job, the more satisfied they are said to be.

Motivation is the inner power or energy that pushes toward acting, performing actions and achieving.

Customer service is the provision of service to customers before, during and after a purchase.

A PRACTICAL GUIDE

KEYS TO A SUCCESSFUL SALES PERSON

1. You got to enjoy what you do.
2. You got like people.
3. You got to like talking.
4. You have to know how to build a relationship.
5. You have to be goal orientated.
6. You have to have endurance.
7. You have to be sensible.
8. You got to have goals.
9. You have to have humour.
10. You have to be respectful.
11. You have to have passion.
12. You have to have determination.
13. You have to have integrity.
14. You have to have a short memory.
15. You have to have a personal philosophy.
16. You have to be honest.
17. You have to be an over comer.
18. You have to be a leader.
19. You have to be a good team member.
20. You have to be physically fit.
21. You have to be inspirational.

22. You have to be professional.
23. You have to know how to read body language.
24. You have to be community minded.
25. You have to be organized.

PRACTICAL KEYS TO SELLING

1. Know and understand your product.
2. Sell a principal with your product.
3. Memorize your script to selling your product.
4. Do role play. Being a seller and buyer. Practice makes perfect.
5. Use a diary to track your movements and sales.
6. Learn how to control the sale. Get them to tell you it is a good product.
7. Learn how to engage your customer. Selling is not telling.
8. Know how to close a sale. Never ask a closed question that demands a no or yes response.
9. Assume the sale. Always Be Closing (ABC).
10. Know how to record and report a sale.

ENEMIES TO SELLING

1. Fear of rejection.
2. Lack of confidence.
3. Lack of product knowledge.
4. Procrastination – assassination of motivation.
5. Lack of motivation – lazy.
6. No vision.
7. No plan, no organization.

8.   Bad personal appearance.
9.   Bad personal hygiene – bad breath.
10. Bad attitude.

DETERMINE YOUR CONSUMERS

By Kay Balbi; The five types of consumers:

"Consumers can be grouped into the following 5 categories: Suspects, Prospects, First time buyers, Repeat buyers and Non-buyers, based upon where they are in the buying process.

Suspects are people that aren't even thinking about buying, prospects are those that are thinking about it, first time-buyers have decided they are going to buy, repeat buyers have bought before, and non-buyers are never going to buy."

http://www.ehow.com/list_6737828_5-types-consumers_.html#ixzz15b9ceIsH

Determine which types you are dealing with to save time and money.

BIBLIOGRAPHY

Extracts from Wikipedia, the free encyclopaedia
http://en.wikipedia.org

Aristotle (384 BC – 322 BC) was a Greek philosopher and polymath, a student of Plato and teacher of Alexander the Great. His writings cover many subjects, including physics, metaphysics, poetry, theater, music, logic, rhetoric, linguistics, politics, government, ethics, biology, and zoology. Together with Plato and Socrates (Plato's teacher), Aristotle is one of the most important founding figures in Western philosophy. Aristotle's writings were the first to create a comprehensive system of Western philosophy, encompassing morality, aesthetics, logic, science, politics, and metaphysics.

Bertrand Arthur William Russell, 3rd Earl Russell, OM, FRS (18 May 1872 – 2 February 1970) was a British philosopher, logician, mathematician, historian, and social critic. At various points in his life he considered himself a liberal, a socialist, and a pacifist, but he also admitted that he had never been any of these in any profound sense. He was born in Monmouthshire, into one of the most prominent aristocratic families in Britain.

Charles Haskell Revson (October 11, 1906 – August 24, 1975) was a pioneering cosmetics industry executive who created and managed Revlon through five decades

Charles Michael Schwab (18 February 1862 – 18 October 1939) was an American steel magnate. Under his leadership, Bethlehem Steel became the second largest steel maker in the United States, and one of the most important heavy manufacturers in the world.

Confucius (551–479 BC) was a Chinese teacher, editor, politician, and philosopher of the Spring and Autumn Period of Chinese history. The philosophy of Confucius emphasized personal and governmental morality, correctness of social relationships, justice and sincerity. His followers competed successfully with many other schools during the Hundred Schools of Thought era only to be suppressed in favor of the Legalists during the Qin Dynasty. Following the victory of Han over Chu after the collapse of Qin, Confucius's thoughts received official sanction and were further developed into a system known as *Confucianism*.

Dan Brent Burt (1952 -) is an American business executive who wrote a number of bestselling books *Selling the IBM Way; Who Killed Service; or Time and Territory Management.*

David J. Schwartz (b. September 22, 1970) is an American science fiction and fantasy writer, whose book Superpowers was a finalist for the Nebula Award.

Dr. Norman Vincent Peale (May 31, 1898 – December 24, 1993) was a minister and author (most notably of *The Power of Positive Thinking*) and a progenitor of the theory of "positive thinking".

Franklin Delano Roosevelt (January 30, 1882 – April 12, 1945), also known by his initials, **FDR** was the 32nd President of the United States (1933–1945) and a central figure in world events during the mid-20th century, leading the United States during a time of worldwide economic depression and total war. The only American president elected to more than two terms, he facilitated a durable coalition that realigned American politics for decades. With the bouncy popular song "Happy Days Are Here Again" as his campaign theme, FDR defeated incumbent Republican Herbert Hoover in November 1932, at the depth of the Great Depression. Energized by his personal victory over paralytic illness, FDR's unfailing optimism and activism contributed to a renewal of the national spirit. He worked closely with Winston Churchill and Joseph Stalin in leading the Allies against Germany and Japan in World War II, but died just as victory was in sight.

Friedrich Wilhelm Nietzsche (October 15, 1844 – August 25, 1900) was a German philosopher, poet, poet, cultural critic and classical philologist. He wrote critical texts on religion, morality, contemporary culture, philosophy and science, displaying a fondness for metaphor, irony and aphorism.

Gautama Buddha or **Siddhārtha Gautama Buddha** (563 BCE to 483 BCE) was a spiritual teacher from the Indian subcontinent, on whose teachings Buddhism was founded. The word *Buddha* is a title for the first awakened being in an era. In most Buddhist traditions, Siddhartha Gautama is regarded as the Supreme Buddha... of our age, "Buddha" meaning "awakened one" or "the enlightened one." Gautama Buddha may also be referred to as *Śākyamuni*. The Buddha found a Middle Way that ameliorated the extreme asceticism found in the Sramana religions. The time of Gautama's birth and death are uncertain: most early-20th-century historians dated his lifetime as c. 563 BCE to 483 BCE, but more recent opinion dates his death to between 486 and 483 BCE or, according to some, between 411 and 400 BCE.UNESCO lists Lumbini, Nepal, as a world heritage site and birthplace of Gautama Buddha. There are also claims about birthplace of Gautama Buddha to be Kapileswara, Orissa or Kapilavastu at Piprahwa, Uttar Pradesh. He later taught throughout regions of eastern India such as Magadha and Kosala.

Hannah Tatum Whitall Smith (February 7, 1832 – May 1, 1911) was a lay speaker and author in the Holiness movement in the United States and the Higher Life movement in the United Kingdom of Great Britain and Ireland. She was also active in the Women's suffrage movement and the Temperance movement.

Henry Ford (July 30, 1863 – April 7, 1947) was an American industrialist, the founder of the Ford Motor Company, and sponsor of the development of the assembly line technique of mass production. His introduction of the Model T automobile revolutionized transportation and American industry. As owner of the Ford Motor Company, he became one of the richest and best-known people in the world. He is credited with "Fordism": mass production of inexpensive goods coupled with high wages for workers. Ford had a global vision, with consumerism as the key to peace. His intense commitment to systematically lowering costs resulted in many technical and business innovations, including a franchise system that put dealerships throughout most of North America and in major cities on six continents. Ford left most of his vast wealth to the Ford Foundation but arranged for his family to control the company permanently.

Malcolm Stevenson Forbes (August 19, 1919 – February 24, 1990) was publisher of *Forbes magazine*, founded by his father B. C. Forbes and today run by his son Steve Forbes.

Mario Gabriele Andretti (born February 28, 1940) is a retired Italian American world champion racing driver, one of the most successful Americans in the history of the sport. He is one of only two drivers to win races in Formula One, Indy Car, World Sports car (the other being Dan Gurney). He also won races in midget cars, and sprint cars. During his career, Andretti won the 1978 Formula One World Championship, four Indy Car titles (three under USAC-sanctioning, one under CART), and IROC VI. To date, he remains the only driver ever to win the Indianapolis 500 (1969), Daytona 500 (1967) and the Formula One World Championship, and, along with Juan Pablo Montoya, the only driver to have won a race in the NASCAR Sprint Cup Series, Formula One, and an Indianapolis 500. No American has won a Formula One race since Andretti's victory at the 1978 Dutch Grand Prix. Andretti had 109 career wins on major circuits.

Melvin Russell Ballard, Jr. (born October 8, 1928) is a religious leader in The Church of Jesus Christ of Latter-day Saints. He was called to serve in the church's Quorum of the Twelve Apostles in 1985. As a member of the Quorum of the Twelve, Ballard is accepted by the church members as a prophet, seer, and revelator. Currently, he is the sixth most senior apostle among the ranks of the Church.

Muhammad (c. 570 – c. 8 June 632); also transliterated as *Mohammad,* or *Muhammed*; full name: *Abū al-Qāsim Muḥammad ibn ʿAbd Allāh ibn ʿAbd al-Muṭṭalib ibn Hāshim* was a leader from Mecca who unified Arabia into a single religious polity under Islam. He is believed by Muslims and Bahai to be a messenger and prophet to God, and by most Muslims as the last prophet sent by God for mankind. Muhammad is generally considered to be the founder of Islam, although this is a view not shared by Muslims. Muslims consider him to be the restorer of an uncorrupted original monotheistic faith of Adam, Noah, Abraham, Moses, Jesus and other prophets.

Oliver Goldsmith (10 November 1730 – 4 April 1774) was an Anglo-Irish writer and poet, who is best known for his novel *The Vicar of Wakefield* (1766), his pastoral poem *The Deserted Village* (1770), and his plays *The Good-Natur'd Man* (1768) and *She Stoops to Conquer* (1771, first performed in 1773). He also wrote *An History of the Earth and Animated Nature*. He is thought to have written the classic children's tale *The History of Little Goody Two-Shoes*, the source of the phrase "goody two-shoes".

Paul Harold Dunn (April 24, 1924 – January 9, 1998) was a general authority of The Church of Jesus Christ of Latter-day Saints (LDS Church). Dunn was widely considered one of the most dynamic speakers among the general authorities in the 1970s and 1980s. In 1991, Dunn stated that he had "not always been accurate" in his speeches and writings after questions were raised about the truthfulness of some of the personal experiences he had included in his writings and his speeches.

Peter Ferdinand Drucker (November 19, 1909 – November 11, 2005) was an influential writer, management consultant, and self-described "social ecologist."

Plato (424/423 BC – 348/347 BC) was a Classical Greek Philosopher, mathematician, student of Socrates, writer of philosophical dialogues, and founder of the Academy in Athens, the first institution of higher learning in the Western world. Along with his mentor, Socrates, and his student, Aristotle, Plato helped to lay the foundations of Western philosophy and science.

Publius Vergilius Maro (October 15, 70 BC – September 21, 19 BC), usually called *Virgil* or *Vergil* in English, was an ancient Roman poet of the Augustan period. He is known for three major works of Latin literature, the *Eclogues* (or *Bucolics*), the *Georgics*, and the epic *Aeneid*. A number of minor poems, collected in the *Appendix Vergiliana*, are sometimes attributed to him. Virgil is traditionally ranked as one of Rome's greatest poets. His *Aeneid* has been considered the national epic of ancient Rome from the time of its composition to the present day.

Ralph Waldo Emerson (May 25, 1803 – April 27, 1882) was an American essayist, lecturer, and poet, who led the Transcendentalist movement of the mid-19th century. He was seen as a champion of individualism and a prescient critic of the countervailing pressures of society, and he disseminated his thoughts through dozens of published essays and more than 1,500 public lectures across the United States.

Ralph Waldo Emerson (May 25, 1803 – April 27, 1882) was an American essayist, lecturer, and poet, who led the Transcendentalist movement of the mid-19th century. He was seen as a champion of individualism and a prescient critic of the countervailing pressures of society, and he disseminated his thoughts through dozens of published essays and more than 1,500 public lectures across the United States.

Raymond Albert "Ray" Kroc (October 5, 1902 – January 14, 1984) was an American businessman who joined McDonald's in 1954 and built it into the most successful fast food operation in the world. Kroc was included in *Time 100: The Most Important People of the Century*, and amassed a fortune during his lifetime. He owned the San Diego Padres baseball team from 1974 until his death in 1984. Similar to another fast-food giant, KFC founder Harlan Sanders, Kroc's success came late in life when he was past his 50th birthday.

Robert Collier (April 19, 1885 – 1950) was an author of Self Help, and New Thought metaphysical books in the 20th century.

Robert Louis Balfour Stevenson (13 November 1850 – 3 December 1894) was a Scottish novelist, poet, essayist, and travel writer. His most famous works are *Treasure Island*, *Kidnapped*, and *Strange Case of Dr Jekyll and Mr Hyde*.

Roberto Críspulo Goizueta (November 18, 1931 – October 18, 1997) was Chairman, Director, and Chief Executive Officer (CEO) of The Coca-Cola Company from August 1980 until his death in October 1997.

Samuel Langhorne Clemens (November 30, 1835 – April 21, 1910), better known by his pen name *Mark Twain*, was an American author and humourist. He is most noted for his novels, *The Adventures of Tom Sawyer* (1876), and its sequel, *Adventures of Huckleberry Finn* (1885), the latter often called "the Great American Novel."

Scott McNealy (born November 13, 1954) is an American business executive. He co-founded computer technology company Sun Microsystems in 1982 along with Vinod Khosla, Bill Joy, and Andy Bechtolsheim.

Sir Arthur Charles Clarke, CBE, FRAS, Sri (16 December 1917 – 19 March 2008) was a British science fiction author, inventor, and futurist, famous for his short stories and novels, among them *2001: A Space Odyssey* (1968), and as a host and commentator in the British television series *Mysterious World*. For many years, Robert A. Heinlein, Isaac Asimov, and Clarke were known as the "Big Three" of science fiction.

Sterling Welling Sill (March 31, 1903 – May 25, 1994) was a general authority in The Church of Jesus Christ of Latter-day Saints (LDS Church). He was an Assistant to the Quorum of the Twelve Apostles from 1954 to 1976 and was a member of the First Quorum of the Seventy from 1976 to 1978. In 1978, he received general authority emeritus status.

Vincent Thomas "Vince" Lombardi (June 11, 1913 – September 3, 1970) was an American football coach. He is best known as the head coach of the Green Bay Packers during the 1960s, where he led the team to three straight league championships and five in seven years, including winning the first two Super Bowls following the 1966 and 1967 NFL seasons. The National Football League's Super Bowl trophy is named in his honor. He was enshrined in the NFL's Pro Football Hall of Fame in 1971.

Warren Edward Buffett (born August 30, 1930) is an American business magnate, investor, and philanthropist. He is widely considered the most successful investor of the 20th century. Buffett is the chairman, CEO and largest shareholder of Berkshire Hathaway and consistently ranked among the world's wealthiest people. He was ranked as the world's wealthiest person in 2008[5] and as the third wealthiest person in 2011. In 2012, American magazine *Time* named Buffett one of the most influential people in the world.

Walter Percy Chrysler (April 2, 1875 – August 18, 1940) was an American automotive industry executive and founder of the Chrysler Corporation.

William Sprague IV (September 12, 1830 – September 11, 1915) was the 27th Governor of Rhode Island from 1860–1863, and U.S. Senator from 1863–1875. He participated in the First Battle of Bull Run during the American Civil War.

Wikipedia website, hosted by the privately incorporated, **nonprofit organization**, Wikimedia Foundation that is governed by a board of trustees. It is a **collaboratively edited**, **multilingual**, **free Internet encyclopedia**. **Volunteers** worldwide collaboratively write Wikipedia's 30 million articles in 287 languages, including **over 4.5 million** in the **English Wikipedia**. Anyone who can access the site can edit almost any of its articles, which on the **Internet** comprise the largest and most popular general **reference work**. In February 2014, *The New York Times* reported that Wikipedia is ranked fifth globally among all websites stating, "With 18 billion page views and nearly 500 million unique visitors a month..., Wikipedia trails just Yahoo, Facebook, Microsoft and Google, the largest with 1.2 billion unique visitors."

ABOUT DEREK

Derek has been in the sales business for 20 years. He has trained hundreds of new aspiring sales people in his field. He has empowered many more to become full time sales people.

Derek is the founder of Adventure Marketing Ltd, an internet and door to door sales company. He also started Ucountcard Ltd and (TPC) Psychology and (DGM) Derek Grace Motivation. Derek resides in Tauranga New Zealand.

NOTES

For further information contact

derekmbc@gmail.com